FOOD
MACHINE

Alan MacDonald

Illustrated by Julian Mosedale

OXFOI
UNIVERSITY I

1
Carlo's birthday party

The Festival of Lights was coming and the village of Bellini talked about nothing else. There was going to be music, dancing and lights in every street.

Carlo was more excited than anyone. Saturday was his birthday and he was having his own party. Everyone would be there. It was going to be the best street party in the village.

'What are you making for my party on Saturday?' he asked his mum.

'Carlo! I've told you a hundred times,' sighed Mrs Rondo.

'Tell me again!' Carlo begged.

'I'm making fried chicken, lemon cake, ice-cream...'

4

'And pizza!' cried Carlo. 'We must have pizza! Your pizza is my favourite!'

'Don't worry,' smiled his mum. 'I won't forget.'

His mother was the best cook in the world. The street party was going to be the best the village had ever seen. What could go wrong?

2

The lights go out!

But on Monday evening, everything *did* go wrong.

Carlo was watching TV. Suddenly it went off and so did every light in the house.

'Mama!' cried Carlo. 'What's happened?'

'It must be a power cut,' said his mum. 'All the electricity's gone off.'

Carlo looked out of the window and saw it was true. The whole village was in darkness.

Mrs Rondo frowned. 'It's very odd. We've never had a power cut before.'

There were no lights, no TV and, worst of all, no way to cook. Mrs Rondo's old oven ran on electricity.

'When will the power come back on?' asked Carlo. 'We'll still have my party, won't we? You'll be able to make your special pizza?'

'Don't worry, Carlo,' said his mum. 'The power will be back on tomorrow.'

But on Tuesday morning, the power was still off. Carlo was worried. The great party was only four days away. Without electricity, there would be no lights across the street. What would they eat, if his mother couldn't cook? What if the power cut spoiled everything?

On his way home from school, Carlo stopped in the village square. A red truck was parked there.

Two men were puffing and wheezing as they lifted something heavy out of the back. One was short and round as a pumpkin and the other was thin as a beanstalk.

Carlo watched as the thin one beat on a drum.

9

Soon a large crowd gathered to see what was happening.

'My friends,' smiled the brothers, 'today is your lucky day. We have brought you a wonder …'

'A marvel!'

'A machine that will change your lives!'

Then the thin one pulled off a sheet,
and there was a dazzling silver machine
with rows of lights and buttons.

'Oooh!' everyone cried.

So did Carlo.

'What is it?' he called out.

'This, my boy, is the Fabulous Food
Machine,' said the plump brother.

'What would you like to taste?' cried the thin one. 'Pizza? Peaches and cream?'

'Pizza!' shouted Carlo.

'Pizza it is! Stand back and watch!'

The thin brother pressed a red button. The machine whirred and rumbled into life, lights flashing on and off.

clunk!

There was a *beep* and a *clunk* and something dropped into a hole at the bottom.

'Ahhhh!' cried the crowd.

It was a green cube. 'You see!' said the plump brother. 'Now, who would like to taste it?'

'I would!' shouted everyone.

'There is one problem,' said the thin brother. 'Only the BEST cooks can taste how truly delicious it is. If you have never tasted wonderful food – well, I'm afraid you won't be able to taste this!'

Carlo's mum was chosen to taste the green cube. She popped it into her mouth and began to chew.

'Well? Can you taste that wonderful pizza?' asked the brothers.

'The melting cheese …

The sweet tomatoes …

The spicy sausage …

That perfect, crispy crust?'

Carlo's mother chewed. To tell the truth, the cube tasted a bit like sawdust. But she remembered what the brothers had said. Only the best cooks could taste how delicious the cubes were. She didn't want people to think that she wasn't a good cook.

So she said, 'Mmm, delicious! Just like my home-made pizza!'

'Of course it is!' said the two salesmen. 'And best of all, this fabulous machine doesn't need electricity. It runs on batteries. Just switch it on, push a button and *clunk*, your favourite food is ready!'

Carlo wasn't so sure. A green cube couldn't be as good as his mum's cooking. But the rest of the village was very happy.

'What luck!' they said. 'Who cares about the power cut? Now we can eat whatever we want!'

Everyone wanted to buy a machine, and Carlo's mum bought the last one.

'Just wait, Carlo,' she said. 'This machine will give us the best food we have ever had!'

3

The Fabulous Food Machine

That evening, Mrs Rondo took out the new machine.

'What would you like to eat?' she asked.

'Pasta and meatballs!' cried Carlo.

His mum pressed the red button. The machine whirred and rumbled and the lights flashed. *Beep! Clunk!* A brown cube fell into the hole at the bottom. Mrs Rondo put a cube on each plate and handed them round. There was one for Carlo, one for Grandpa and one for herself.

The family ate their supper in silence. In a few seconds it was gone.

'Mmm! Delicious!' said Mrs Rondo. 'Did you taste the meatballs? That spicy sauce?'

'Very nice,' nodded Carlo's grandpa, glumly.

Carlo didn't say anything. He thought the cubes tasted horrible – like sawdust.

The power cut went on – and on.
Alberto from next door was the village
policeman.

He told Carlo that someone had cut
through an electricity cable. It would
take days to mend it.

The villagers ate green, blue or
brown cubes for breakfast, lunch and
supper. No one was brave enough to
say that they tasted of sawdust. They
were afraid that everyone would think
they had never tasted good food!

Friday came.

'Mama,' said Carlo. 'What are we eating at my party tomorrow?'

Mrs Rondo sighed. 'I've told you a million times, Carlo. We'll have your favourite pizza.'

'You mean real pizza, or pizza from the machine?' asked Carlo.

'From the machine, of course.'

'Oh,' said Carlo sadly. He didn't want to eat horrible green lumps on his birthday. He wanted real food – his mum's special pizza. How he wanted to give that stupid machine a good kick!

'What's the matter, Carlo?' asked Grandpa.

'Nothing,' sighed Carlo. 'But I told everyone my party would be the best in the village.'

'I know,' said Grandpa.

'But it *won't* be,' said Carlo. 'How can you have a party without lights or good food!'

Carlo stumped up the stairs to his room and Grandpa shook his head.

21

4

What is your favourite food?

On Saturday morning, Carlo woke up bursting with excitement. It was his birthday. Then he remembered the power cut. Without power, his mother couldn't cook and his party would be ruined.

He opened his presents. His mum gave him a football. He got a model police car from Alberto next door.

Grandpa's present was his mum's old cookbook, tied up with a red ribbon.

'Thanks, Grandpa,' said Carlo, trying to sound happy.

'What do you think of your present?' asked Grandpa.

'It's fine,' said Carlo.

'Maybe it's better than it looks. Let's open it.'

Carlo turned the pages. The pictures made him feel hungry.

'Tell me, Carlo. What is your favourite food?' asked Grandpa.

'That's easy! Mama's pizza!' said Carlo. 'What's *your* favourite food, Grandpa?'

'I'll show you,' replied Grandpa. He pointed to a picture.

'Steak,' he said. 'Sizzled in a pan.'

'Mmm!' said Carlo. 'I wish we could eat one.'

'Maybe we can,' said Grandpa. 'Why don't we pop next door? I think Alberto should see your book, too.'

Carlo showed Alberto the cookbook. For a long time, he turned the pages.

'Alberto,' said Carlo. 'What is your favourite food?'

Alberto sighed deeply. 'Nothing beats fried chicken, Carlo. I wish I could taste it again.'

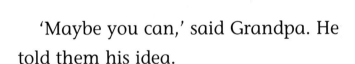

'Maybe you can,' said Grandpa. He told them his idea.

Soon, Alberto was grinning happily.

'I'll come at seven,' he said, 'and I'll bring what I need.'

'Don't be late,' said Grandpa.

'I wouldn't miss this for anything,' said Alberto.

At seven o'clock everyone started to arrive.

Mrs Rondo looked out of her window. '*Santa Maria!* What is going on, Carlo?' she cried. 'We can't feed all these people!'

'Don't worry, Mama,' laughed Carlo. 'There'll be plenty to go round.'

Carlo was right. News of the party had spread through the village. Everyone had come – and they had all brought their favourite food.

There were huge hams, sacks of rice, boxes of vegetables and armfuls of bread and fruit. The street was lit by hundreds of flickering candles.

Grandpa set up six barbecues, ready for cooking. Then they fried chicken, sizzled steaks and boiled up bubbling pans of pasta. Mrs Rondo even baked her special pizza in a tin!

At last, when everyone had eaten as much as they could, Alberto got to his feet. 'My dear Carlo,' he said. 'Thank you for this party! Thank you for giving us back our food!'

Then everyone sang 'Happy Birthday'.

'Well, Carlo?' asked Grandpa as they went to bed. 'Was it a good birthday party?'

Carlo grinned from ear to ear.

'Thanks, Grandpa. It was the best day of my life!'

5

The end of the story

On Sunday morning, Mrs Rondo threw her Fabulous Food Machine out of the house. All over the village, people did the same. The machines sat by the dustbins, dusty and unwanted.

At ten o'clock the power came back on. Alberto called round later to tell them all about it. He said two brothers had been arrested for cutting through an electricity cable. One of them was plump as a pumpkin and the other thin as a beanstalk.

'The rotten cheats!' gasped Carlo's mum. 'They cut off our power to make us buy their stupid machines!'

'Have you locked them up, Alberto?' asked Carlo.

'I have, Carlo,' smiled Alberto. 'But they won't go hungry. They get a brown cube for breakfast, a blue one for lunch and a green one for supper!'

About the author

Perhaps you know the story of *The Emperor's New Clothes*? It tells how a foolish emperor is tricked by two tailors, who pretend to make him an 'invisible' suit.

In this story, I've given the tale a new twist and the trickery is about a wonderful food machine. Eating seems to come up a lot in my stories. My own favourite meal is hot steaming pasta – better than a green cube, any day!